Riding the Rails in the USA
Trains in American Life

Transportation in America

Riding the Rails in the USA
Trains in American Life

Martin W. Sandler

OXFORD
UNIVERSITY PRESS

This book is dedicated to the thousands of railroad buffs across America who, through their love of steam and rail, have kept the story of a vital part of the nation's life alive.

Acknowledgments

I wish to thank Carol Sandler, Karen Fein, and Nancy Toff for all the help and encouragement they have given me. Thanks are also due to Amy Richter for her valuable suggestions and to Alexis Siroc for her excellent design of the book. Finally I am grateful for having Nancy Hirsch as my editor. Her editing skills are but part of the many contributions she has made to this book.

Picture Credits

Courtesy of Amtrak: 57; B+O Railroad Museum: 8; Courtesy of Chuck Donaldson: 58; Duke University Library: 20, 39; Library of Congress: cover, frontispiece, 1, 2, 9, 12, 17, 18, 21, 23, 24, 26, 29, 31, 32, 33, 35, 36, 40, 41, 43, 46, 47, 48, 51; Courtesy of Thurman Naylor: 44, 49; Courtesy of Ringling Bros. And Barnum & Bailey: 54; Sandler Collection: 11, 45; University of Washington Library: 15, 30.

OXFORD
UNIVERSITY PRESS

Oxford   New York
Auckland   Bangkok   Buenos Aires   Cape Town   Chennai
Dar es Salaam   Delhi   Hong Kong   Istanbul   Karachi   Kolkata
Kuala Lumpur   Madrid   Melbourne   Mexico City   Mumbai   Nairobi
São Paulo   Shanghai   Singapore   Taipei   Tokyo   Toronto

Copyright © 2003 by Martin W. Sandler

Design by Alexis Siroc

Published by Oxford University Press, Inc.
198 Madison Avenue, New York, New York 10016
www.oup-usa.org

Oxford is a registered trademark of Oxford University Press

Library of Congress Cataloging-in-Publication Data

Sandler, Martin W.
  Riding the rails in the USA : trains in American life / Martin W. Sandler.
     p. cm.
Summary: Explores the impact of trains in the United States as they allowed settlers to move West in large numbers and get needed supplies, helped farmers to move goods to market, and provided transportation for commuters.
Includes bibliographical references and index.
  ISBN 0-19-513228-9 (alk. paper)
  1. Railroads—United States—History—Juvenile literature. [1. Railroads—History.]
I. Title.
  HE2751 .S26 2003
  385'.0973—dc21   2002014155

9 8 7 6 5 4 3 2 1

Printed in Hong Kong on acid-free paper

COVER: A train with its huge steam locomotive dominates this illustration of the variety of 20th-century transportation.

FRONTISPIECE: A mid–19th century train makes its way across a bridge in Niagara Falls, New York.

Contents

CHAPTER 1

The Coming of the Rails

"For every traveler ten years ago, there are a hundred now, and we are sometimes fearful [the railroads] will make us a nation of travelers, always in motion, and that the art will be brought to such perfection that it will be cheaper to travel than to stay at home and pay rent...."

—*New York Herald*, 1852

"When I hear the iron horse make the hills echo with his snort like thunder, shaking the earth with his feet, and breathing fire and smoke from his nostrils," wrote American author and philosopher Henry David Thoreau, "it seems as if the earth had got a race now worthy to inhabit it." The iron horse Thoreau was speaking about was the train. This new invention, unrivalled until the coming of the automobile in the early 1900s, provided Americans with previously unknown speed and reliability in moving about from one place to another over land. Yet, important as they were, speed and reliability were but two of the benefits that Americans discovered in the train.

The railroad's ability to transport people to places once reached only by courageous pioneers in their horse- and ox-drawn wagons made it possible for Americans in great numbers to populate the West. The fact that the train could transport huge quantities of freight over long distances became in many ways more important to the nation than its more celebrated ability to carry passengers. Manufacturers in the East not only found important new markets in the West but were able to have much-needed raw materials delivered to them by rail from the western lands, which were rich in natural resources. And the train made it possible for farmers all across the country to send the fruits of their labor to new and more distant markets.

The railroad, which by 1910 became the nation's largest employer, spawned whole new industries and boosted the fortunes of those that had already been established. Iron and steel, for example, used both in the rails and in the building of locomotives and railroad cars, became two of the United States' largest manufactures. As the railroad continued to grow it also became the leading catalyst for scientific and technological developments. Scores of other industries adopted many of those innovations. Automobile manufacturers, for example, modeled their electric headlights after those that the railroads developed in the 1880s. Later, the airline industry would take advantage of the advancements in braking systems that the railroads had achieved.

Perhaps the railroad's greatest achievement was the way it changed people's sense of time and space. A person traveling by stagecoach from Omaha, Nebraska, to San Francisco, California, in 1865, for example, needed to allow up to two months for the journey. After the first transcontinental railroad was completed in 1869, the trip was reduced to six days. By 1888 trains were moving people across the continent so rapidly that it became necessary to replace the different time zones under which individual states operated with four standard zones for the nation.

More than anything that had come before it, the railroad spoke directly to the nation's love of freedom of movement, a trait that is deeply ingrained in the American character.

All of this is not to say that the story of the rise of the American railroad was without its share of problems and injustices. The railroads came to be owned by a few enormously wealthy men, known as the "robber barons." By crushing all competition, owners such as Cornelius Vanderbilt and Jay Gould were able to charge unjustly high rates, particularly in the shipping of farm produce and other freight. Immigrant laborers built

Peter Cooper earned his fortune as a glue maker and a real estate speculator while building his locomotive, *Tom Thumb*. The 1830 race between Cooper's train and a horse called Lightning proved to railroad owners that locomotives would soon replace horses.

Riding the Rails in the USA

many of the nation's railroad lines. At a time of deep racial and ethnic prejudice, these workers, particularly those who had been recruited from China, were often made fun of and treated badly by their fellow laborers. They were also paid less than their co-workers.

The railroad also had a devastating effect on the Native Americans of the West. As the trains brought more and more settlers into the region, the displacement of those who had been first on the American land accelerated greatly. As many of these settlers crossed the Indians' hunting grounds by train, they discovered a new sport: shooting buffalo from the trains' open windows and rear platforms. So many buffalo were killed in this frivolous manner that the Indians, who relied on the buffalo for their meat and hides, found this vital source of survival rapidly fade away.

In 1808, 17 years before he constructed his tiny steam train, John Stevens had built one of America's first steamboats. Although it ran only on a small, circular track, Stevens's train helped prove that steam-propelled travel by rail was possible.

But despite these drawbacks, the railroad played an essential role in the building of the United States. As President John F. Kennedy reminded us in a speech to a railroad organization, "...it was the railroads that bore the great tide of Americans to the areas of new opportunities and hope. It was the railroads that linked together the diverse elements of this vast land so that together they might create the greatest economy the world has ever known."

The beginnings of modern railroading go back to the ancient Greeks. About 2,000 years ago they built roads that had stone blocks with grooves in them. They hauled goods over these roads in horsedrawn wagons that had wheels that fit into the grooves. In about 1500, miners in Germany came up with a better idea. Instead of grooved roads, they hauled carts filled with the minerals they took from the mines along wooden rails. Crude as both these systems were, they inspired a whole new notion of transportation. Before long, inventors and tinkerers began to realize that they could develop a dramatic new form of overland transit if they could invent some type of engine to supply power to propel cars over rails.

They found their answer in the steam engine, first manufactured by the Scottish inventor James Watt in 1774. The leading pioneer in the use of steam power in the United States was a man named Oliver Evans. In 1804 he built a steam engine that was lighter and capable of supplying more power than any previous device of its kind. Evans was a visionary who believed that one day the steam engine would move people over land faster over greater distances than had ever been thought possible. As early as 1813, he predicted that steam-driven carriages, moving over rails, would travel "almost as fast as birds fly, fifteen or twenty miles an hour." Evans even envisioned the laying down of double tracks so that "carriages may pass each other in different directions. . . ." He also imagined trains would be able to "travel by night as well as by day; and [that] the passengers will sleep in the stages as comfortably as they now do in the steam boats."

John Stevens of Hoboken, New Jersey, built the first steam locomotive to run on rails in the United States. It was a tiny engine, really more of a toy train than a vehicle. In 1825 Stevens ran his engine on a circular track on his New Jersey estate. Four years later, an English-built locomotive named the *Stourbridge Lion* became the first full-sized steam locomotive to run on American rails. A canal company used it to haul coal from a Pennsylvania mine to the construction site of a new canal.

In order to finance the huge cost of laying their tracks, purchasing their locomotives, and extending their lines, railroad owners sold stock in their companies. Stock certificates such as this one for the Buffalo and Susquehanna Railroad have become collectors' items.

After the *Stourbridge Lion* experience, it was clear that a lighter locomotive was needed, a feat accomplished by an inventor named Peter Cooper. In

After the canal was completed, the *Stourbridge Lion* was purchased by the owners of the Delaware and Ohio railroad, one of the nation's earliest railroads. But it proved to be too cumbersome to negotiate the curves on that company's track, which had originally been built to accommodate horse-drawn, trolley-like vehicles known as horsecars.

1830, Cooper built a much smaller locomotive, the first ever to transport passengers in America. Because of its small size, it was nicknamed the "Tom Thumb." On August 25, 1830, Cooper successfully ran his locomotive, pulling a passenger-filled, boat-shaped car behind it, along the 13 miles of track on the Baltimore and Ohio horsecar line. About halfway through Cooper's

Whether they were large city terminals, like this one in Chicago, or small rural depots, railroad stations provided the setting for fond farewells and hearty welcomes.

return trip, the driver of a horse-drawn car on the adjacent track challenged him to a race. People had been informed that such a challenge would be made and the track was lined with spectators. As the primitive train and the horsecar raced toward the finish line, the *Tom Thumb* pulled steadily ahead. Suddenly, a belt on the primitive locomotive slipped, causing the train to lose power and the race. But railway owners had seen enough to become convinced that the iron horse would soon replace the real horse in carrying Americans over the rails.

By 1840 several railroad companies had been formed, most notably the Baltimore and Ohio in Maryland and the Charleston and Hamburg in South Carolina. They had laid more than 3,200 miles of track, which was wider and much sturdier than the track used by the horsecar lines. Trains were now beginning to run on regular schedules. Yet although these early railroads represented a revolution in overland transportation, they also presented real challenges to those who traveled on them. After making a short journey by train, English author Charles Dickens described a ride on an American railroad as "a great deal of jolting, a great deal of noise, a great deal of wall, not much window, a locomotive engine, a shriek and a bell." He neglected to mention the thick smoke and soot from the steam engines that commonly choked and blinded passengers or the sparks flying from the engine that often burned holes in passengers' clothing.

Some of the loudest criticism of the early railroads came from individuals concerned not with their lack of comfort but with what they felt the railroad would do to the nation's morals, health, and behavior. Some ministers railed from their pulpits, protesting that traveling at speeds of up to 20 miles per hour went against what the Lord had planned for mankind. There were doctors who told their patients that the human body was incapable of traveling at such speeds, and that serious physical as well as mental ailments would result, including the boiling of one's blood.

The criticisms did little to stop people from boarding the trains. By 1850, both locomotives and the cars they trailed behind them had been greatly improved. More than 9,000 miles of track ran in every direction throughout the East. "For every traveler ten years ago," wrote the *New York Herald*, "there are a hundred now, and we are sometimes fearful [the railroads] will make us a nation of travelers, always in motion, and that the art will be brought to such perfection that it will be cheaper to travel than to stay at home and pay rent. . . ."

As the trains made their way through the still predominately pastoral landscape, the distinctive sound of the locomotive whistle became a source of national pride. For many, the railroad was the very symbol of American progress, the key to a future that held nothing but promise. No one expressed these feelings more eloquently than the American poet Walt Whitman. To Whitman, the railroad was the "type of the modern! emblem of motion and power! pulse of the continent!"

CHAPTER 2

Linking the Nation

"If those of future times should seek for a day on which the country became a nation it may be that they will not select the outcome of some political campaign or battle field, but choose instead the hour when two engines—one from the East and the other from the West—met at Promontory Point."

—*Deseret* (Utah) *News,* 1869

By 1865, scores of American railroad companies had been established and had extended eastern railroad lines as far west as the Mississippi River. A few had even reached out into the Nebraska Territory. Thousands of miles of track had also been laid on the nation's West Coast, but most of them ran north and south. Between the lines in the East and those on the West Coast lay a gap of more than 1,700 miles.

It was into this gap that American pioneers kept pouring in ever-increasing numbers. Railroad company owners saw an enormous opportunity in the seemingly endless migration. They were aware that there were millions of potential travelers who would eagerly grasp the opportunity to make the journey to the new western territories by train rather than by covered wagon or oxcart. They also knew that once these territories were settled and towns and even cities were built, there would be millions of people who would use the trains to travel from one spot in the new regions to another. The railroad owners looked forward to the prospect of the flow of factory-made products from the East and agriculture from the West that their trains would transport.

The railroad tycoons were not the only ones who wished to bring the trains across the nation. Many federal and state government officials shared their desire. The notion of transcontinental railroads was not new. As early as the 1840s, some railroad owners and private citizens had envisioned the day when several lines would link the nation from coast to coast. In the 1850s the major railroad companies began sending teams of surveyors from the Mississippi River all the way to the Pacific coast to determine which routes would be most feasible.

The surveying crews' task was extremely difficult. The vast lands west of the Mississippi were filled first with hundreds of miles of open prairie, then miles of empty desert, and then towering, seemingly impassable mountains. All along the way there were rivers to be crossed.

As the American railroad played an increasingly important role in the building of the West, the train became a leading symbol of American progress. This illustration, "Madonna of the Rails," appeared on the title page of the Milwaukee Railroad's guidebook titled *Across the Continent*.

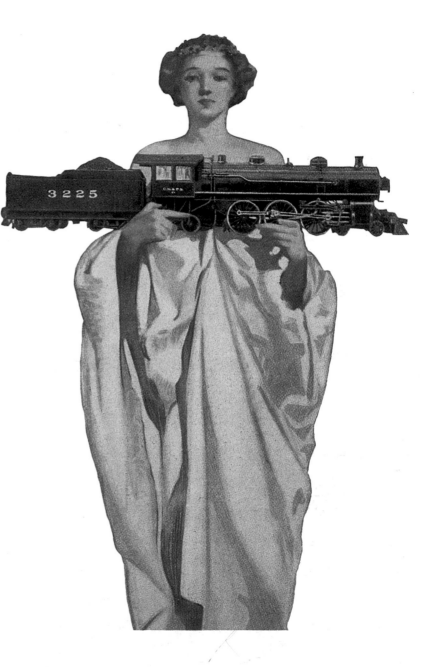

The survey teams succeeded in mapping out several possible routes. In 1862 President Abraham Lincoln selected one of these routes and authorized the construction of the nation's first transcontinental railroad. At this time, however, the United States was in the throes of its Civil War, so the 1,775-mile project was delayed until 1865, when the conflict finally ended and two railroad companies were awarded contracts to begin construction.

These two companies were the Union Pacific, which would lay its tracks westward out of Omaha, Nebraska, and the Central Pacific, which would set down its rails eastward from Sacramento, California. Because their contracts called for them to be paid according to how many miles of track they laid, an intense rivalry grew up between the companies.

From the start, it was obvious that the Union Pacific would have an enormous advantage. Much of this railroad's designated route westward would take it across the flat, open lands of the Great Plains. The Central Pacific, however, would have to forge its way through the wide mountain ranges and across the scorching deserts of the far western lands. But even with the Union Pacific's advantage, the project presented both companies with challenges that no construction crews had ever faced.

"At one time," the Union Pacific's chief engineer Grenville Dodge would later write in his memoirs,

> we were using at least 10,000 animals, and most of the time from 8,000 to 10,000 laborers. The bridge gangs always worked from five to twenty miles ahead of the track. . . . To supply one mile of track with materials and supplies required about forty cars. [On] the plains everything—rails, ties, bridging, fastenings, fuel . . . and supplies for men and animals . . . had to be transported from the Missouri River. Therefore as we moved westward, every hundred miles added vastly to our [difficulties].

Surveying crews worked hundreds of miles ahead of the track-laying gangs, mapping out the exact route to be followed. Other crews, working with pick axes, shovels, and horse- or mule-drawn graders, smoothed out the roadbed and prepared it for the laying of the tracks. Behind them came the bridge builders, whose job was to

Chinese workers pose beside a plow used to remove snow after one of the many blizzards during the building of the first transcontinental railroad. "Although every appliance was used to keep the road clean from snow..." stated Union Pacific official Alfred Brown in a report to his company, "it was impossible to keep it open over half the time and that mostly by means of men and shovels."

The precision with which the tracks were set into place was a marvel of efficiency. "Thirty seconds to each pair of rails...three blows to each spike, ten spikes to a rail, 400 rails and 4,000 spikes and 12,000 blows to a mile. To every mile some 2,500 ties," wrote the *Deseret News*. The constant clanging of steel hammers against steel spikes created an unforgettable sound. "It is a grand Anvil Chorus that those sturdy sledges are playing across the plains," exclaimed another author, William Bell, as he observed the track layers in action.

erect trestles across the many rivers and gullies that lay along the route. Behind the bridge monkeys, as they were called, came the horse-drawn wagons loaded with the long, heavy, wooden ties upon which the tracks would be laid. Finally came the men who would lay the tracks.

Locomotives from the Union Pacific and the Central
Pacific met at Promontory Point, Utah. "The engineers
ran up their locomotives until they touched..." wrote
Union Pacific official Grenville Dodge in his memoir,
"and thus the two roads were wedded into one great
line from the Atlantic to the Pacific."

Riding the Rails in the USA

As track layers set each section of rails in place, the long work train that served as supply carrier, dormitory, blacksmith shop, and dining hall to all the laborers followed closely behind. A heavy locomotive pushed the work train. At its front, a flatcar carried all of the tools needed in the railroad's construction. Behind it, three 85-foot-long boxcars each contained three tiers of bunks in which the men slept at night. Behind the sleeping cars came the dining car with its long table at which 125 men could be fed at one time. The last car in the work train was partitioned into three sections housing the kitchen, the storeroom, and the engineers' office.

For the better part of six years, the construction crews of the Union Pacific and the Central Pacific worked their way toward each other. Even the most optimistic in each company had known from the beginning that laying track across the western wilderness would not be easy. No one, however, had ever imagined just how difficult it would be.

For one thing, neither of the two companies was prepared for winter on the Great Plains and in the western mountains. During the winter of 1866–67, the West experienced no fewer than 44 blizzards. The wind blew so ferociously that the snow on the prairie piled up in 40-foot drifts, often entirely halting the progress of the Union Pacific crews. "Although every known appliance was used to keep the road clear from snow that winter, including the largest and best snow plows then known," Union Pacific official Arthur Brown later recalled, "it was found impossible to keep it open over half the time and that by means of men and shovels, which required an army of men on hand all the time at great expense."

As difficult as the blizzards made it for the Union Pacific, storms presented even greater challenges for the Central Pacific laborers working in the western mountains. One of these storms lasted 13 days and dumped 10 feet of snow on the Central Pacific's route. In order to try to keep the work going, the company built what may have been the largest snowplow ever constructed. Some 30 feet long, it was attached to a special car and pushed by 12 locomotives. The drifts still could not be budged.

Enormous amounts of blasting powder finally solved the problem.

After experiencing the blizzards of 1866–67, in which avalanches killed a number of workers, both railroad companies realized that they would have to take measures to counteract the fierce storms certain to occur while laying their track in winter months. In areas particularly prone to heavy drifting, they erected long, crude, wooden, tunnel-like "snowsheds," which protected both the workers and the tracks from mounting snows. To observers, these "snowsheds," built all along the far western route of the railroad, became familiar landmarks of the great construction adventure.

The weather was but one of the many challenges to be met, particularly by the Central Pacific work crews. Laying tracks through the mountains was, in many ways, the greatest challenge of all. In case after

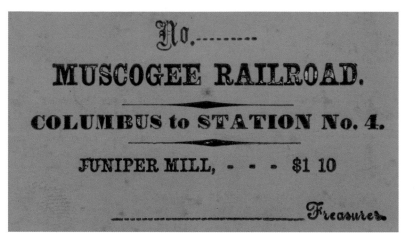

No.---------

MUSCOGEE RAILROAD.

COLUMBUS to STATION No. 4.

JUNIPER MILL, - - - $1 10

_____ *Treasurer*

As the train became the main method of overland travel in America, hundreds of different railroad companies were formed. This railroad ticket was from the Muscogee Railroad, which in 1853 began running trains between Columbus, Georgia, and Macon, Georgia.

case, the only way through the natural barriers was by blasting tunnels. The most difficult tunneling feat was the creation of the Summit Tunnel in Nevada, which was carved through 1,659 feet of solid granite in a mountain that rose 7,032 feet above sea level. To build the tunnel, laborers used some 500 kegs of blasting powder a day. Despite this unprecedented use of blasting materials, work in punching through the tunnel progressed at only eight inches a day.

Although the majority of laborers on the transcontinental railroad were Irish immigrants, many of the men who were responsible for blasting the way through the mountain ranges were Chinese workers,

The Underground Railroad

By 1861, the year in which the Civil War began, railroads had become the nation's best means of overland transportation, and railroad terminology was widely used in various areas of the nation's life. A prime example was the use of the term "Underground Railroad" to describe the way slaves were secretly brought out of the South to freedom in the North. The Underground Railroad was not actually a railroad. It has been said that the term was first used by a slave owner who, having lost the trail of his escaped slave, stated, "He must have gone down an underground road."

Soon railroad terminology was being used for all aspects of the effort to aid escaped slaves. Those who owned slaves were called "agents." Escaped slaves were hidden at "stations" and those who helped them on their flight north were called "conductors." The slaves themselves were referred to as "passengers." Although most escaped slaves were spirited away in horse-drawn wagons or made their way to freedom on foot, some, with the help of abolitionists (those against slavery), were hidden in crates and sent north on trains.

$100 REWARD!

RANAWAY

From the undersigned, living on Current River, about twelve miles above Doniphan, in Ripley County, Mo., on 2nd of March, 1860, A NEGRO MAN, about 30 years old, weighs about 160 pounds; high forehead, with a scar on it; had on brown pants and coat very much worn, and an old black wool hat; shoes size No. 11.

The above reward will be given to any person who may apprehend this said negro out of the State; and fifty dollars if apprehended in this State outside of Ripley county, or $25 if taken in Ripley county.

APOS TUCKER.

Supported by men and women known as abolitionists, African Americans held in bondage fled slavery via the Underground Railroad. Slave owners responded by offering rewards to anyone who would aid in the capture of a "runaway."

hired by the Central Pacific. Beginning in 1865, the company commissioned agents to travel to China to recruit laborers. The Central Pacific advanced money for their passage to the United States, which it later deducted from their wages.

Initially, thousands of the Chinese were put to work with picks, shovels, and wheelbarrows, grading the route upon which Central Pacific tracks would be laid. But because the Chinese were generally smaller and more nimble than the other workers, they were particularly adept at climbing the face of tall cliffs through which tunnels or passageways had to be constructed. Bearing drills and sledges, Chinese workmen were lowered from the top of the cliffs by ropes attached to wicker baskets. As they swayed in the wind, often banging against the side of the cliffs, they bore holes in the rock and inserted blasting powder. When their task was completed, they were hauled up out of range of the ensuing blast. "If it were not for the Chinese," claimed one Central Pacific official, "this road would never be completed." Aside from their

courage and agility, one of the reasons the Chinese workers were limited to the most dangerous jobs had to do with the racist attitudes held by railroad owners.

The cruel weather, the hazards of the mountain barriers, and various types of illnesses killed more than 200 railroad workers. Still, the two companies moved relentlessly forward. By May 1869, the Union Pacific, in its drive westward, had put 1,066 miles of track in place. The Central Pacific had laid down 689 miles of rails. It became clear that the long-awaited connection point was to be high in the Rocky Mountains of Utah. After much debate, both companies decided that the tracks would meet on May 10, 1869, at a place 56 miles west of Ogden called Promontory Point.

Railroad officials carefully planned the festivities that would mark the linking of the rails. Workmen from both companies would join together to lay the last 100 feet of track. Then three ceremonial spikes would be driven into the ties that secured the rails, signifying that the long construction project was at last completed. The first of these spikes, donated by Nevada, was made

A Union Pacific poster announces the opening of the first transcontinental railroad line. "The railway," stated *Frank Leslie's Illustrated Newspaper* in 1881 "has so [condensed] time and space, that...we have almost ceased to speak of the frontier."

of silver. The second, from Arizona, was iron, silver, and gold. The final spike, donated by California, was made of pure gold and engraved with the prayer, "May God continue the unity of our Country as the Railroad unites the two great oceans of the world."

There was a fourth spike as well. Partially driven into a special tie, it was wired into the national telegraph system and into bells and cannon located throughout the nation. At the moment that Leland Stanford, the president of the Central Pacific, drove his special hammer, also wired, onto the final golden spike, a telegraph operator would send the news throughout the nation.

All across the country, thousands of people gathered at telegraph offices and in the streets awaiting the signal. Back in the western mountains, some 600 spectators drew close to the final section of track. The telegraph operator sent out a preliminary message: "Almost

The immediate success of the nation's first transcontinental railroad inspired many companies to construct cross-country lines. This 1870s map shows the route of the Atlantic and Pacific Railroad Company's line.

ready. Hats off. Prayer being offered." The workmen lifted the last rail onto the roadbed. But as they did so a photographer shouted to his assistant, "Shoot." The laborers dropped the rail and ran for their lives.

When order was restored and the last section put into place, Leland Stanford stepped up to the golden spike. "All ready now," wired the telegraph operator. Stanford raised his hammer, took a mighty swing—and completely missed the spike. The telegraph operator, however, did not wait for a second attempt. His simple message "Done" raced across the wires, and almost instantly bells rang and cannon boomed in cities from coast to coast. Many of these celebrations went on for days. Recognizing the importance of the achievement, poet and author Bret Harte wrote,

> What was it the Engines said,
> Pilots touching head to head
> Facing on a single track
> Half a world behind each back?

The celebrations were well founded. For what had once been thought impossible had been achieved: The nation had been linked by two bands of steel.

CHAPTER 3

The Train in the West

"A journey over the Plains was [once] a formidable undertaking that required great patience and endurance. Now all is changed…the six months' journey is reduced to less than a week. The prairie schooner has passed away, and is replaced by the railway coach."

—*Frank Leslie's Illustrated Newspaper,* 1870

Less than a week after the ceremonies at Promontory Point, regularly scheduled trains of the Union Pacific–Central Pacific line were racing across the country. Tourists, anxious to see firsthand the wonders of the American West, filled the trains. But the roster of passengers was made up of far greater numbers of people seeking to settle the western lands.

In order to encourage the railroad companies to bring their tracks into the West, the government had given them enormous tracts of land which they, in turn, could sell to the settlers. The railroads' holdings measured more than 1.5 million acres. That was considerably more than all the land in New England. Determined to sell as much land as possible and to lure future rail travelers into the area, the railroads flooded areas east of the Mississippi with newspaper advertisements, posters, books, and pamphlets, all aimed at luring people to the West. None of these advertisements and literature mentioned the droughts, blizzards, backbreaking work, and other challenges that faced all those who wished to build a new life in the West. Instead, they portrayed the western lands as a carefree paradise.

On journeys across the country that could take up to five days, passengers on the new transcontinental lines encountered astounding sights, such as herds of buffalo and prairie fires.

The Northern Pacific Railroad, for example, encouraged settlement of the land it owned by claiming that the air in its western territory was so healthy that it could cure almost every type of ailment. Advertisers filled most of the ads, posters, and pamphlets with overstated claims of the ease with which crops could be grown and the huge profits to be gained.

Along with targeting farmers in the rocky-soiled East, the advertising campaigns were aimed at the millions of the nation's factory workers who worked from sunup to sundown for meager wages. These ads ignored the fact that farming the western lands required even longer hours of toil. Instead, they emphasized the benefits of working in the open air as opposed to toiling in the stifling factories.

The ambitious advertising campaigns were not confined to the United States. The railroads sent agents to nations throughout Europe. Their job was to entice European peasants, almost all of whom had never had the chance to own land, to come to the United States and start life anew in the West. The agents promised that they would arrange for the immigrants to purchase land in easy payments. They also offered cheap steamship passage to the United States and inexpensive train travel to the West.

Railroad agents also worked in the American seaports where immigrants arrived. Their job was to change the minds of the new arrivals who were planning to live in American cities and convince them to settle in the railroads' western lands.

The advertising campaigns and the persuasive powers of the agents were highly successful. Throughout the 1870s and 1880s, tens of thousands of farmers, factory workers, and new immigrants climbed aboard trains and headed for the West. By the time these western newcomers were being carried over the rails, comfortable, even elegant railroad cars had been designed. Most immigrants, however, could not afford such luxury. The cars that transported them to the West were stripped of all but the simplest necessities. They were equipped with nothing but rows of wooden benches upon which two people could sit. At night, every other row was turned around, boards were set across the facing seats, and straw-filled cushions were laid upon them. Two people could lay side by side on these "beds" and attempt to get some sleep.

The immigrants took all their meals on their journey at dining counters at stations along the way. The dining rooms in these stations were crowded places with people shouting their food orders to the harried counter staff. Since the train was apt to pull out of the station with almost no warning, the travelers had to gulp their food and at the same time look out the window to keep an eye on the train. Some immigrants complained that during their entire journey to the West, they never got to finish one meal.

But even for those western settlers who could afford to take only the trains charging the lowest fares, the trip to the West was dramatically different from the journey by covered wagon experienced by earlier pioneers. "A journey over the plains," exclaimed a correspondent for *Frank Leslie's Illustrated Newspaper,*

> was [once] a formidable undertaking that required great patience and endurance. Now all is changed. The shriek of the locomotive wakes the echoes of the slopes along the Sierras, through the cañons of the Wasatch and the Black Hills, and his steady puffing is heard as he creeps along the mountain sides. The six months' journey is reduced to less than a week. The [covered wagon] has passed away, and is replaced by the railway coach.

The trains were responsible for doing much more than filling up the once untamed western lands with settlers. By making it possible for people from every section of the country to visit one another, the trains united the nation in a way that few would have thought possible just a decade earlier, when the Civil War divided the country. "The changes now taking place," stated United States President James Garfield in a speech to Congress, "have been wrought and are being wrought, mainly, almost wholly, by a single mechanical device, the steam locomotive. The railroad is the greatest centralizing force of modern times."

By the 1880s, four other transcontinental railroads—the Northern Pacific, the Great Northern, the Southern Pacific, and the Atchison, Topeka and Santa Fe—had been constructed. As the tracks for these long-distance lines—and the shorter lines that branched off from them—were laid, hundreds of towns sprang up in their wake. "The railroads are the true roads of America," stated *Frank Leslie's Illustrated Newspaper.* "They have made the towns, and the towns turn to

Farm produce is loaded onto a train in Ohio for shipment to the East. By allowing farmers to expand their market, "the railroad," reported *Harper's Weekly* in 1884, "has given the burdened farmers a whole new lease on life."

The guidebooks published by the railroad companies to lure passengers to the West featured articles and illustrations of western scenery and train travel. On this cover of the Northern Pacific Railroad's guidebook, the American eagle and a woman symbolizing liberty float over beautiful western vistas.

them in grateful acknowledgment, not banishing them to the back regions, but receiving them in their very midst."

Along with widely scattered small towns that the earliest pioneers had established, many of the first towns in the West were those that sprung up along the path of the first transcontinental railroad. Rough places, often filled with hard-drinking men, they had been built to cater to the needs of the construction crews. When the crews completed their work and moved on, many of these places turned into "ghost" towns.

However, most of the towns that grew up along the western lines, once these lines were established, survived and prospered. Some of these towns the railroad companies had planned and initially constructed (like the small town that became Chicago). Others spontaneously sprouted up. The railroad put the people in these towns in touch with the world. It made travel from one place to another easy. It meant that the town's stores could be stocked with all kinds of goods, brought by the train. It meant goods produced in the town could be shipped almost anywhere.

In most cases the towns that were established along the railroads eventually spread out physically on both sides of the tracks. Out of this grew an interesting social system. In most towns there came to be what was regarded as the "right side" and the "wrong side" of the tracks, determined by which way the wind blew sooty smoke from the trains' locomotives. The side that most frequently had to endure the smoke became the wrong side, the site of the town's factories, simpler stores, and less expensive houses. The right side of the tracks, or what was generally the smokeless side, became the locale of the town's expensive shops, churches, and higher-priced homes.

The trains not only brought settlers to the West and created many of the communities in which people lived; they also had a profound effect on the way work was carried out in the vast western territories. The great majority of pioneers, for example, had come to the West to earn their living by farming the land. With the

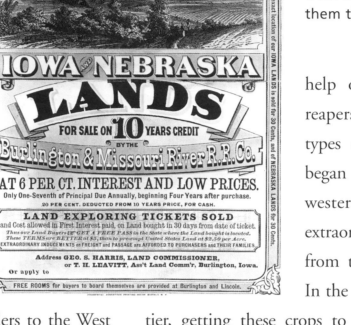

Railroad companies advertised "millions of acres" of inexpensive land for sale and hoped to convince settlers to move to the West with pictures of beautiful scenery and discounts on the train tickets that would get them there.

help of mechanical planters, reapers, threshers, and other types of farm machinery that began to appear in the 1870s, western farmers produced extraordinary amounts of crops from the fertile western lands. In the earliest days on the frontier, getting these crops to market was one of the biggest challenges of all. The trains solved this problem. As freight trains came to dominate the way goods were carried in and out of western territories, the fruits of the farmers' labor could be shipped to market over even the longest distances.

TEN MINUTES FOR REFRESHMENTS.

Artists had a field day depicting the way early trains to the West paused only briefly for hungry passengers to refresh themselves. "Ten minutes for refreshments" was an exaggeration, but to travelers, a scene like this one was all too familiar.

The train not only established a key role for the western farmer, it was a major influence in the work of the most legendary of all western figures, the American cowboy. The cowboys' work involved raising herds of cattle, rounding them up every spring, and then leading them over long trails to railroad centers as many as 1,800 miles to the north. There, in places such as Dodge City, Ellsworth, and Abilene, Kansas, the cowboys placed the cattle in freight cars that transported the animals to Chicago and cities in the East where they were butchered.

The crops raised on the prairie and carried by train to American markets and to ports from which they were shipped overseas helped feed most of the nation and many foreign countries. Included in these crops were several new varieties of grains introduced on the prairie. By creating what became known as the "bread-basket of the world," the pioneer farmers established themselves as the true heroes of the West.

In the 1880s, that all changed. As the railroads began to fan out across Texas, Arizona, Colorado, and the other cattle-raising states, it was no longer necessary for cowboys to trail cattle long distances to railroad centers. Trains made up of cattle cars came right to where the animals were raised. The animals were then loaded onto the cars and transported directly to the slaughterhouses. With the cattle drives eliminated, far fewer cowboys were needed. It was an ironic develop-ment. The train, which in the 1870s and early 1880s had been a major factor in the rise of the booming cattle industry, had become a key factor in the ending of the cowboy's glory days.

By the end of the 1880s, the railroad had brought more than 5 million people into the West. Towns and cities were flourishing. Stores in these communities were filled with the most up-to-date merchandise, all brought in by rail. In 1890 the U.S. officially declared that the West could no longer be regarded as a frontier area. Thanks in great measure to the train, the nation had been truly linked.

The $100 first-class fare from Omaha to San Francisco entitled passengers to all the luxuries provided by the Pullman dining cars, parlor cars, and sleepers. Immigrants who paid $40 and rode on cramped board seats enjoyed no such luxuries, but *The Modern Ship of the Plains*, as this drawing is titled, provided a rapid, inexpensive way to begin a new life in the West.

CHAPTER 4

The Train Comes of Age

"Music sounds upon the prairie and dies away far over the plains. Merry-making and jokes, conversation and reading pass the time pleasantly until ten o'clock when we retire."

—*Harper's Weekly* correspondent
traveling in a Pullman parlor car, 1881

By 1910, the 92 million people in the United States lived in a nation that had developed an enviable railroad system. Not only did the United States possesses two-thirds of all the railroad track in the world (almost 250,000 miles of rails), but continual improvements in locomotives, cars, and other railroading equipment had made American trains safer and more comfortable than ever before.

The early railroads had given their passengers a frightening ride. Choked and even burned by the constant barrage of smoke and sparks that flew out of the locomotives' steam engines, many travelers swore that their first journey on a train would be their last. Beginning in the late 1850s, numerous new types of smokestacks were invented and installed on both wood-burning and coal-burning locomotives. Sporting names such as Diamonds, Shotguns, Capstacks, Sunflowers, and Balloons, these variously shaped smokestacks helped prevent showers of sparks from falling on the train or igniting the surrounding countryside.

At the same time, the railroads began to take advantage of the telegraph, which Samuel F. B. Morse

The danger signal, one of many railroad safety devices developed in the late 1800s, was credited with preventing scores of accidents. By giving off a loud, shrill noise, the signal enabled the locomotive engineer to warn others of his approach.

had invented in 1844. Railroad telegraph operators aided passengers by wiring ahead to the stations in which they waited, advising them whether or not their train would be on time. Most important, operators were able to send messages to the trains themselves and warn the engineers of any dangerous obstacles that lay on the tracks ahead of them.

From the time that the first railroad lines were built in the United States, owners had sought a way to operate their trains safely at night. The earliest lines were forced to shut down completely when darkness fell. Anxious to keep its cars moving around the clock, New

Jersey's Camden and Amboy line tried a novel experiment. It placed a flatcar filled with burning timber in front of one of its locomotives and had the locomotive push the flatcar ahead of it to illuminate the way. A foolhardy and dangerous idea, it was quickly abandoned.

What did work, however, was the installation of oil lanterns on locomotives. A metal shield mounted behind the lantern's flame directed light ahead of the engine to penetrate the darkness. The oil lanterns were

In the late 1890s and the early 1900s, many American trains provided luxuries rivaled only by those found in the most expensive hotels. The *New York Times* reported that travelers sped "twenty-seven miles in twenty-seven minutes" without spilling a drop of their champagne.

not very bright. However, the trains of the 1830s and 1840s traveled only at speeds of up to 20 miles per hour, and these first headlights proved adequate.

By the end of the 1850s, kerosene headlamps had replaced oil lanterns and provided considerably more light. The real breakthrough took place in the early 1880s, shortly after electricity was perfected. The first electric locomotive headlights were installed in 1883, providing enough light for the trains, which by that time were racing along the tracks at more than 70 miles per hour.

CHICAGO & ALTON R

THE GREAT
PALACE RECLINING-CHAIR ROUTE
Between CHICAGO AND KANSAS CITY
CHICAGO AND ST. LOUIS AND
ST. LOUIS AND KANSAS CITY
FREE OF EXTRA CHARGE AND WITHOUT CHANGE
J. C. McMULLIN • C. H. CHAPPELL • JAMES CHARLTON • GEO. J. CHARLTON

PALACE DINING CARS

PULLMAN PALACE Buffet Sleeping CARS

Until Eli H. Janney introduced the first effective device designed to connect the cars in a train together, the danger of cars on a speeding train becoming separated was all too real. Early railroad cars were linked together by chains, which made for uncomfortable stops and starts. It was a dangerous method as well, since the constant jerking of the chains made them apt to break. An improvement was made in the mid-1850s, when the link-and-pin coupling system was introduced. In this system, iron housings with holes on either side were mounted on railway cars. A heavy iron pin was inserted through the holes, to connect the cars together. This reduced the jerking brought about by the train's starts and stops. However, it was extremely dangerous for brakemen who had to hold the pins in place while the locomotives brought the heavy cars close enough to be linked. Several brakemen had their hands crushed when they failed to pull them away fast enough after inserting the coupling pin.

All of this changed in 1868 when Janney introduced his automatic coupler. The Janney coupler worked like two hands clasping together. When the two couplers were brought together the "hands" closed. Then a linking pin could safely be inserted. In 1893, federal laws mandated that all trains be equipped with automatic couplers. Janney's invention is still vital to railroad operations, although in today's couplers the linking pin is automatically inserted when two couplers come together.

Another improvement came about in an unusual way. In the 1840s, a speeding locomotive crashed into a cow that had wandered onto the tracks. The locomotive was severely damaged, and the company was ordered to pay for the cow that had been killed. After other cows were killed in a similar manner, railroad inventors developed a large, iron, scoop-like structure that was attached to the front of the locomotive. This simple device, naturally called a "cow catcher," became a distinguishing feature of steam locomotives. Cow catchers proved to be invaluable in cushioning the shock experienced when trains bumped into rocks, tree limbs, or the many other objects that fell onto the tracks.

The new types of smokestacks, improved head lamps, the automatic coupler, the cow catcher, and the use of the telegraph all were vital railroad improvements. No safety advancement, however, was more important than the development of the air brake. When the driver of a locomotive in the early 1830s approached a station where he needed to stop, he shut off the engine's power, causing the train to come to a crawl. A railroad employee at the station would place himself in front of the train, dig in his heels, and brace his hands against the front of the locomotive. At the same time, another employee would thrust a fence rail between the spokes of one of the locomotive's wheels.

By the mid-1830s, this dangerous and unreliable system was replaced by another idea. Sturdy blocks of wood, connected to foot pedals inside the locomotive and the cars, were placed near the train's wheels. When the pedals were pushed they pressed against the wheels, bringing the train to a halt.

The wooden brakes were more effective than the earlier method of braking but were still far from satisfactory. Despite continued efforts by inventors and engineers, no truly effective way of bringing a train to a halt was found until George Westinghouse developed the air brake.

Westinghouse got the idea for his new type of braking system when he read a story about Swiss engineers who were successfully cutting a tunnel through thick rock by using the powerful force supplied by compressed air. Westinghouse devised a system in which pistons driven by compressed air pressed metal plates against the wheels of a train with such force that the train would be brought to an immediate halt.

Westinghouse was only 22 years old when he patented his air brake in 1872. His invention got an early test when one of the first trains to be equipped with the brakes rounded a curve and came upon a wagon that had stalled on the tracks. The air brakes stopped the train before it smashed into the wagon. Still, many railroad owners were skeptical of the revolutionary new system. When Westinghouse tried to convince Commodore Cornelius Vanderbilt, one of the most powerful of the railroad tycoons, to equip his many trains with the new air brakes, he scoffed at the idea. "Do you pretend to tell me that you could stop trains with the wind?" asked Vanderbilt. "I'll give you to understand, young man, that I am too busy to have any time taken up in talking to a damned fool."

Westinghouse, however, refused to be discouraged. He kept improving his braking system, and by the mid-1870s, almost all trains were equipped with his air brakes. A pioneer in the use of recently invented electricity, Westinghouse also made another vital railroading contribution by inventing the first practical electric safety signals. Through the use of colored lights mounted on poles, Westinghouse's signals warned engineers when to slow down and indicated when it was safe to speed

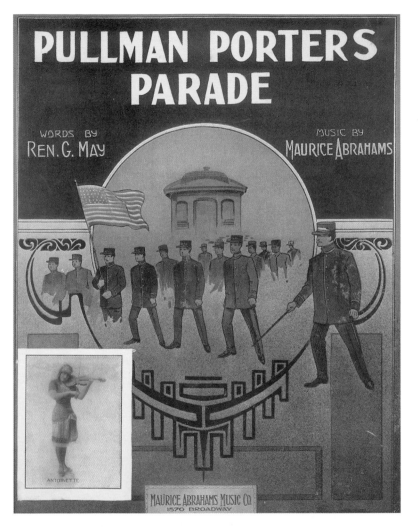

Pullman porters served passengers by bringing them drinks and newspapers, making their beds, and ensuring they were as comfortable as possible. The words to this song in their honor began "Here they come down the street / Just see those Pullman Porters."

up. The signals, installed at railroad crossings, also warned pedestrians and the drivers of horse-drawn vehicles of the approach of an oncoming train.

While inventors like George Westinghouse and Eli H. Janney devoted themselves to making train travel safer, other innovators were developing ways to make the journey by train, particularly on the six-day transcontinental routes, more comfortable. Even before the first transcontinental line was built, George Mortimer Pullman had developed hinged seat-backs that could be laid out flat, enabling passengers traveling significant distances at night to get their sleep. Once the transcontinental lines were established, Pullman introduced his Pullman Palace Cars. Passengers who could afford the fare could travel and sleep in unprecedented comfort.

The demand for space on the Palace Cars was so great that only a year after the first transcontinental railroad was completed, the Union Pacific ran at least three of the cars on each of its long trains. "I had a sofa for myself, with a table and a lamp," wrote one passenger in *Harper's Weekly*. "The sofas are widened and made into beds at night. My berth was three feet, three inches wide and six feet, three inches long. I had two windows looking out of the train, a handsome mirror, and was well furnished with bedding and curtains."

Some Pullman Palace cars even had organs. In the evening during the trip, traveling musicians or talented amateurs would entertain passengers as they were whisked across the country. "Music sounds upon the prairie and dies away far over the plains," the *New York Times* quoted one passenger as saying. "Merry-making and jokes,

The comfort and speed delivered by the luxury trains provided an almost irresistible lure for travelers. By the mid-1890s, thanks in part to the marvelous meals served on the Union Pacific's route between Omaha and Sacramento, some 1 million passengers a year were traveling on this one line alone.

conversation and reading pass the time pleasantly until ten o'clock when we retire."

Pullman also introduced the dining car, which appeared on transcontinental trains in the late 1880s. The dining cars were lighted with beautiful lamps and were lined in rich mahogany. Gourmet chefs prepared the meals and highly trained waiters served them on

the finest china. Many first-class passengers were so well fed they boasted of having happily gained weight during their journey.

All of the improvements in railroading safety and comfort were seen as examples of American ingenuity and pride in workmanship. But at the same time, there was a serious social issue in the nation, one in which the railroads played a central role. Many railroad companies that operated in the South segregated their cars into those for white passengers and those for black travelers. In 1896 a Louisiana black man named Horace Plessy sued the railroad companies after he was denied a seat in a "whites-only" car.

In a case that became famous as *Plessy* v. *Ferguson*, the U.S. Supreme Court ruled in favor of the railroads stating that such segregation was legal as long as sep-

Describing the introduction of Pullman sleeping cars in 1864, the *Baltimore Chronicle* reported that "nothing now seems to be wanting to make railway travel perfect and complete in every convenience." British author Charles Dickens, however, did not agree. After traveling in one of the early sleepers he wrote to a friend that "to tell you that these beds are perfectly comfortable would be a lie."

arate facilities (in schools and other facilities as well as railroad cars) for blacks were as good as the facilities for whites. For the next 58 years, even though the facilities for blacks were never nearly as good as those for whites, this "separate but equal" policy became standard practice in the American South. In 1954, in another landmark court case *(Brown* v. *Board of Education)*, this unjust practice was finally abolished with the conclusion that separate could never truly be equal.

CHAPTER 5

Working on the Railroad

"Make no small plans."

—motto of Daniel Burnham,
architect of Washington, D.C.'s Union Station, 1888

As train travel became more comfortable, as new lines continued to appear, and as passenger volume increased, the railroads became the nation's largest employer. By 1910, some 1 million Americans worked for the railroad as tracklayers, signal and switch operators, mechanics, coal men, conductors, engineers, and other jobs. Thousands of these employees were sleeping or parlor car attendants called porters. Almost all these workers were African Americans who, at this time of deep racial discrimination, could only find railroad work in these low-paying jobs.

Of all these employees, those who received the greatest attention were the engineers, the men who drove the trains. In a nation in love with trains, the engineer, who was responsible for keeping tons of speeding locomotives and cars under control, was treated as a hero.

But just as the engineer was first in the hearts of his passengers, he was also first on the scene of a railroad accident. Despite the many improvements that had been made in railway safety, accidents were all too common and often catastrophic.

A crowd in Waco, Texas, gathers to view the results of a spectacular train crash. Before railroad officials and inventors began focusing their efforts on developing safety devices, incredible wrecks like this one were common.

Many of the railway accidents were due to the excessive speeds at which many of the trains traveled. From the days of the stagecoach and the steamboat, Americans had developed a passion for speed. Railroad companies, determined to beat out their rivals in bringing passengers from one point to another, often set schedules that could only be met by engineers pushing their trains to the limit. Another major cause of accidents was railroad bridges, many of which were built of wood, before locomotives and cars became increasingly heavy. Several major accidents took place when wooden bridges collapsed under the weight of a heavy train.

Accidents had been part of railroad history from the very beginning. In 1831, months after the *Best Friend of Charleston,* the first locomotive built in the United States, went into service, it blew up, killing a crewman who had shut down a pressure valve to stop the noise it was making. But early accidents were minor compared to the carnage that took place once trains grew much larger and were able to attain dizzying

One of the most popular magazines for young people in the late 1800s and early 1900s, *Pluck and Luck* romanticized the role of the train engineer—referred to as "The Prince of the Rail"—as action hero.

PLUCK AND LUCK

COMPLETE STORIES OF ADVENTURE.

No. 12.   NEW YORK, June 15, 1898.   Price 5 Cents.

ENGINEER STEVE, THE PRINCE OF THE RAIL. BY JAS C. MERRITT.

STEVE

There is no stopping now, no turning back! It is all or nothing! Like a flash the engine clears the intervening space, and with an increased impetus leaps the gap! Not the tenth part of a second is occupied in making the awful leap.

speeds. And it was those whose job it was to be continually aboard the trains—the engineers, the conductors, the dining and sleeping car attendants—who were most often the victims.

In 1888, the first year in which official records of railroad accidents were compiled, 2,070 railroad men were killed and 20,248 others were injured. "I discovered," one new railway employee told the *New York Times,* "that it was taken as a matter of course that railroad men of necessity be maimed and killed."

Some of the railroad disasters became legendary through song and story. The lyrics commemorating what became known as the Chatsworth Wreck of 1887 were typical of the songs that became familiar to shocked but spellbound Americans.

> A mighty crash of timber,
> The sound of hissing steam,
> The groans and cries of anguish,
> A woman's stifled scream
> The dead and dying mingled,
> With broken beams and bars
> An awful human carnage—
> A dreadful wreck of cars.

The many instances in which engineers lost their lives made them even bigger heroes in the minds of the American public. The dangers they faced and the heroics that they sometimes performed combined to give a few of them, like John Luther "Casey Jones," legendary status.

Casey Jones gained his fame and lost his life on the night of April 30, 1900. Driving his train, the *Cannonball Express,* at more than 65 miles per hour, Jones suddenly spotted a stalled freight train on the tracks dead ahead of him. As his fireman (the person shoveling coal into the train's steam engine) jumped from the cab to avoid being killed in the impending crash, he shouted for Jones to do the same. But Casey knew that if he did so the *Cannonball Express* would hit the freight train at full speed. Instead, he hung on and slowed his train down as best he could. Although the crash killed him, his actions greatly reduced the number of other lives that might have been lost. The song commemorating his deed, which began, "Come all you rounders if you want to hear, the story told about a brave engineer," remains one of the most familiar of all railroad songs.

The greatest number of employees who worked for the railroad were

The men who drove the locomotives worked long, hard hours, often without any breaks. This engineer's wife waits for his train to pass by a designated spot in Proctor, Vermont, so she can hand him lunch.

not those who rode the trains or maintained them. They were the tens of thousands of men and women who worked in the railroad stations, or depots as they were often called, throughout the nation. These workers included agents, announcers, custodians, baggage handlers, and ticket sellers.

The main purpose of railway stations was to serve as the boarding and disembarking place for passengers. But they were far more than that. In small towns across

The train affected almost every aspect of American life, including politics. American Presidents and Presidential candidates such as Calvin Coolidge found that campaigning from the back of a train enabled them to reach out personally to voters across the nation.

the nation, the railroad depot was the heart of the community, the place where people gathered, often on a daily basis. They not only watched the trains come and go, but gossiped and exchanged news and pleasantries with their neighbors.

It was in the cities, however, that the railroad stations reached their zenith. As train traffic continued to increase, almost every major city hired a renowned architect to build a station that would outshine those in other urban centers. By the late 1880s and early 1890s, these builders had incorporated a variety of classical architectural styles and had erected structures of extraordinary grandeur.

The cities of St. Louis, New York, Boston, Detroit, Chicago, and Philadelphia, as well as Worchester, Massachusetts, and Louisville, Kentucky, built gigantic railroad stations. Dramatic rooflines, gables, windows, and towers characterized them all. Arguably the most dramatic was the terminal erected in St. Louis. This station featured a wide, elegant concourse that led to an enormous platform where 23 different railroad companies backed up their trains.

With the elegance of city railroad terminals fully established, railroad owners, city officials, and their architects began turning their attention to maximizing the use of the enormous space within the structures. They launched campaigns to persuade businessmen to locate their establishments within the monumental terminals. The businessmen, aware of the numbers of people who passed through the stations every day, needed little convincing. By 1900, restaurants, shops, theatres, and even hotels filled many of the nation's largest stations. In several cities, plans were made to locate sports arenas either above, below, or adjacent to the terminals, and by 1925 several of these arenas had been built.

Of all American railroad terminals, the greatest marvel was New York's Grand Central Station, which was constructed between 1913 and 1915. Regarded as one of the premier engineering accomplishments of its

PULLMAN Compartment Cars
CINCINNATI, INDIANAPOLIS, CHICAGO.
THROUGH TRAINS
CINCINNATI, DAYTON, TOLEDO, DETROIT.
INTERIOR OF **DINING CARS** ON THE **CINCINNATI, HAMILTON & DAYTON R.R.**

At a time when trains throughout the South were segregated, thousands of African Americans found employment as railroad porters and dining car attendants on the very trains they were not allowed to ride as passengers.

time, Grand Central was really two stations in one. Tracks and waiting rooms belowground served the thousands of passengers who commuted daily to and from New York's many suburbs. Passengers traveling to distant points throughout the nation used waiting rooms and boarded trains that were on tracks at ground level. The multi-level terminal was so large and operated so efficiently that more than 30,000 people could gather inside the station at one time without overcrowding.

When first the automobile and then the jet airliner cut deeply into the number of train passengers, many of the elegant railroad stations were either reduced in size or demolished. Among those that were torn down was New York's original Pennsylvania Station, long one of the nation's most famous railway terminals. Fortunately, there have been some notable exceptions to this demolition. In the late 20th century New York's Grand Central Station, Philadelphia's 30th Street Station, and the palatial railroad terminal in Worcester, Massachusetts, were all beautifully renovated. Grand Central's ceiling, famous for its depiction of the night sky, was painstakingly cleaned. The golden "constellations" were regilded, and the old-fashioned bulbs that gave the ceiling's stars their glow were replaced with modern fiber-optic lights.

Arguably the finest restoration of all has taken place in Washington, D.C.'s Union Station. The terminal's waiting rooms were enlarged and equipped with modern amenities and lighting. New spacious walkways were constructed throughout the massive structure. Escalators were installed between the waiting rooms and ticket counters on the street level and the railroad gates at the level below. The original creation of architect Daniel Burnham, whose motto was "Make no small plans," the station today houses a cinema complex and some of the U.S. capitol's most popular restaurants. With its beautiful lines and its inviting plaza stretched out in front of it, Union Station is a vivid symbol of civic pride and a reminder of the central role the railroad has played in the nation's history.

In many cities during the great days of the railroad, the train station was the most beautiful building in the community. Built in 1908, Washington, D.C.'s majestic Union Station was the largest train station in the world and covered more ground than any other building in the country.

A Model Town

George Mortimer Pullman not only invented the railroad sleeping car but also created a bustling American town. By 1881 the Pullman Palace Car Company had become so large and profitable that Pullman moved his manufacturing plant to Chicago and then built a nearby community to house more than 12,000 of his workers. Named Pullman, Illinois, it earned a reputation as a model community, featuring parks, playgrounds, tree-lined streets, and several churches. In order to maintain the tranquility of the town, Pullman prohibited bars. And in keeping with the racial discrimination that was so prevalent at the time, he would not permit hundreds of African-American porters who worked for him to live in the town.

Pullman, Illinois, became a forerunner of dozens of other company towns that were established by business magnates throughout the country. When Pullman died in 1897, Robert Todd Lincoln, President Lincoln's son, took over as head of the Palace Car firm and overseer of the town.

In the 1890s, workers at Pullman Palace Car Company factories in various locales staged a strike in support of their demand for higher wages. Here, army officers clear the way for a train to pass through demonstrators' lines during an 1894 Pullman strike in Chicago.

CHAPTER 6

New Trains for Modern Times

"My youth was charmed by the glamour of the locomotive. . . . Never did I dream that my career as an artist-engineer would lead me some day to that glorious adventure, the designing of a steam [locomotive]."

—Streamliner designer Raymond Loewy, in his memoirs, 1940

The period between the late 1920s and the early 1940s saw the creation of some of the most distinctive industrial designs ever to appear in the United States. Historians have labeled the design styles "streamline," "moderne," or, most commonly, "art deco."

Almost everything that was made at the time came under the influence of art deco, which emphasized clean, sleek lines and tapered and elegant shapes. These contours were incorporated into products and structures that ranged from toasters and other household appliances to skyscrapers that loomed over American cities.

By the late 1920s locomotives had become more important to American life than ever before. It was not surprising that industrial designers saw in these massive, powerful machines the opportunity to create some of their most spectacular streamlined designs. One of those called upon by the railroads to bring a new, sleek look to trains was the industrial designer Raymond Loewy, who would write in his memoirs in 1940:

My youth was charmed by the glamour of the locomotive. Never did I dream that my career as an artist-engineer would lead me some day to that glorious adventure, the designing of a steam engine. Last year . . . my first streamlined locomotive, developed in collaboration with the engineering department of the Pennsylvania Railroad, was placed in operation. It was an even greater thrill than I had expected. To Engine 3768, my heartiest wishes for a fast and brilliant career.

Engine 3768 was but one of hundreds of streamlined locomotives that designers and engineers created for the railroads. Trim, sleek, and beautifully constructed, they were called "streamliners." And the public loved them.

Determined to take full advantage of the excitement the streamliners were causing, the railroads launched advertising campaigns as extensive as those they had used to sell the western lands they once owned. Those hired to create the ads were instructed to use the word "streamliners" wherever they could and to emphasize not only the beauty but the speed and the comfort of the new trains. Other designers were hired to bring a streamlined look to everything connected

The popularity of the streamliners helped the railroads survive the economic hard times of the Great Depression. Many songs celebrated the beauty and speed of these new diesel-powered trains.

with travel on the new trains—cups, glasses, baggage tags, and the like.

Beginning in the late 1930s, more than 350 of these stainless steel trains—with names such as *Zephyr, Silver Meteor, Super Chief,* and *Twentieth Century Limited*—were racing across the country at speeds averaging almost 80 miles per hour. The introduction of the streamliners ushered in what many now refer to as the golden age of train travel. But a dramatic change in the appearance of many trains was not the only major development of the era. Even more far-reaching were the changes made to the way locomotives were powered.

For more than 100 years, steam had propelled trains. But in the late 1930s, 40s, and 50s, railroad owners replaced their steam engines with diesel engines. The newly perfected diesels were far less expensive to operate and maintain. They could also haul heavier loads of passengers and freight at faster speeds than steam-powered trains.

Whereas steam engines burn wood or coal to heat water into the steam that powers the locomotive, a diesel engine compresses air into a cylinder, then sprays oil into the same cylinder, which the heat of the compression ignites. This supplies the power for the locomotive. A major advantage of diesel locomotives is that in contrast to steam locomotives, which need to be "fired-up" for up to two hours before they can move, diesels can get under way immediately. Another advantage is that diesels do not need the heavy mechanisms beneath the locomotive that the steam engines required, and so cause far less stress on the tracks over which they travel, saving millions of dollars a year in repairs.

Although the majority of railroad owners turned to diesels to drive their trains, some companies replaced their steam locomotives with yet another power source—electricity. Electrical power, supplied either by overhead wires or by an electrified third rail, has some advantages over diesel. Because there are no fuel emissions connected with electricity, it is a much cleaner source of power. And electric locomotives are even less costly to maintain. However, the initial expense of purchasing electric locomotives and constructing and maintaining either overhead wires or electrified rails is so great that the diesel engine became the power source of choice for most American railroads.

By the 1950s, the railroads found themselves confronting whole new challenges. The ever-growing American trucking industry had taken a large share of the freighting business away from the railroads, and jet airliners had been fully developed. As the airlines shrunk time and distance even more dramatically than the fastest streamliners, they lured thousands of travelers away from the trains.

Faced with the stiffest competition they had ever encountered, railroad owners in several nations began to develop bold new types of trains. In 1964 the Japanese

Although both the automobile and the jet airplane have cut deeply into railroad ridership, the train still plays an important role in American life. Millions of people throughout the nation rely on the train to take them to work and back home again.

Ringling Bros. and Barnum & Bailey, the nation's
largest circus, still transports its animals, performers,
and equipment around the country by train.

Riding the Rails in the USA

government introduced the world's first high-speed electric railroad line, named the Tokaido Shinkansen. The so-called Bullet Trains, which continue to run along this line, attain top speeds of up to 131 miles per hour.

Inspired by the Japanese success, other nations followed suit. In the 1980s France began operating its Train á Grand Vitesse (TGV, high-speed trains). In 1990 a new version of the train named the TGV Atlantic became the fastest passenger train in the world, attaining a speed of more than 185 miles per hour. At the same time, high-speed Inter City Express (ICE) lines began carrying passengers between points in Germany. Also in Europe, trains of the Eurostar line, traveling through a long tunnel under the English Channel—the "chunnel"—provide high-speed rail service between London, Paris, and Brussels.

These significant advancements have been conspicuously absent in the United States. One of the reasons is that the United States, more than most countries, cherishes its free-enterprise system, one in which the government stays out of business ventures as much as possible. In 1970, however, in response to increasing public demand for a national high-speed train service and aware that private companies could not afford such a venture, the United States created a rail system which it named the National Railroad Passenger Corporation (known as Amtrak, from the words *American* and *track*).

During its first two decades of operation, this public corporation encountered many problems, particularly the lack of tracks capable of handling high-speed trains. By the early 1990s, however, Amtrak had improved many of its rails. In 2000, Amtrak inaugurated its Acela Express, which began traveling along the United States' northeast corridor at speeds of up to 150 miles per hour.

Although the United States still has much catching up to do in the development of high-speed trains, more than 84 million Americans continue to ride the rails every year. Millions commute to and from work daily by train. Hundreds of thousands of people, wanting to avoid the delays and other hassles often experienced at airports, opt for train travel. And even though jet air travel has cut deeply into rail passenger service, many people use the train to get to and from the air terminals.

Since passenger services between cities are provided by federally owned Amtrak and most suburban commuters travel by railway lines operated by local governments, privately owned railroads earn almost all their money by hauling freight Even during the railroads' busiest years, freight was more profitable than passenger trains. In recent years the development of much faster and more powerful diesel and electric-powered freight locomotives, combined with improved methods of handling cargo, have won freight traffic back from the trucking companies. Every day, for example, the Union Pacific runs more than 125 freight trains across the continent—some more than one full mile in length.

As in the earlier years of railroading, much of today's freight is transported either in boxcars or on flatcars. Boxcars are essentially empty boxes on wheels. Originally 40 feet long, their length has been extended over the years and today many are as long as 85 feet. They are particularly popular with shippers because they can transport many different kinds of freight— anything from live chickens to computers.

The simple flatcar, which is a long, wide platform on wheels, is used to carry large, bulky items such as machinery and lumber. Today, flatcars transport truck trailers filled with goods. Truck drivers bring the trailers to a freight yard where they are loaded onto flatcars. Once the train reaches its destination, other truck drivers hitch the trailers to their cabs and take them to wherever they are scheduled to be unloaded. Known as "piggybacking," this procedure saves trucking companies the time and expense of hauling the trailers long distances over the highways.

Another type of freight car is the refrigerator car, designed to transport perishable goods. First patented in 1868, the early refrigerator cars were cooled by blocks of ice loaded onto the cars at icing stations along the route. When modern refrigeration techniques were developed in the early 1900s, refrigerated cars became

Amtrak's Acela Express, the nation's first high-speed railroad, runs from Boston to New York at over 150 miles per hour, making the trip about 45 minutes shorter than the old Metroliner.

far more efficient. Today, diesel-electric equipment provides refrigeration that can keep goods frozen or cooled for weeks at a time. Other common types of freight cars used today include tank cars, which carry cargo such as liquid chemicals and food products, and hoppers, which transport loose bulk goods such as grain, coal, and iron ore.

New freight cars were created to meet the transportation demands brought about by new kinds of products and by changes in the way modern companies ship freight around the world. The production of automobiles in great numbers, beginning in the 1900s, led to a need for transporting autos from the factories to dealerships throughout the country. Railroad owners responded by introducing the auto-rack car. These railcars have rear doors for easy loading and ramps that permit as many as 18 automobiles to be stacked inside them.

An effective method of shipping goods globally, particularly by ship, is through the use of huge metal containers. As this form of shipping became more common in the late 1950s, the intermodal freight car was developed. The term "intermodal" means that goods can be moved via more than one mode of transportation. Intermodal freight cars carry huge containers filled with all sorts of goods. They transport these containers either to seaports or truck terminals where they are transferred onto ships or trucks without ever having to have their contents reloaded.

By committing itself to upgrading passenger service and by continually developing faster, more powerful, and innovative types of freight trains and cars, the government and privately owned railroad companies are keeping the U.S. railroad tradition alive. The train took up where the steamboat and covered wagon left off, and peopled the nation. By moving goods over land more efficiently and over greater distances than anything that came before, it played a key role in determining the course of both American agriculture and industry. It united the nation both physically and spiritually. Walt Whitman was right. For more than 120 years, the railroad was indeed ". . . [the] pulse of the continent!"

An enormous modern freight train pulled by two powerful diesel locomotives makes its way through an area in Oregon known as the Dalles. As in the days of steam-driven trains, hauling freight remains the railroad industry's largest source of income.

Timeline

1804

American Oliver Evans builds the first successful high-pressure steam engine

1825

John Stevens builds and operates a small steam locomotive on a circular track in Hoboken, New Jersey

1829

First full-sized steam locomotive runs on American railroad tracks

1830

Tom Thumb, built by Peter Cooper, is the first American locomotive to transport passengers

First American-built steam locomotive goes into scheduled passenger service

1840

More than 3,200 miles of track have been laid in the eastern United States

1850

More than 9,000 miles of railroad track now run in every direction in the East

1851

Telegraph is first used for dispatching trains

1857

First Pullman sleeping car, built by George Mortimer Pullman, is put into service

1862

President Lincoln authorizes building of first transcontinental railroad

1868

Eli Janney patents the automatic railroad car coupler

1869

First transcontinental railroad is completed

1870–1874

Four additional transcontinental rail lines completed

1872

George Westinghouse patents the automatic air brake

1880

First trains are equipped with electric lights

1888

Railroads introduce the four standard time zones to the United States

1910

The train transports almost 975 million American passengers a year

1930–1950

Railroad companies replace steam locomotives with diesel for freight and passenger service

1934

Streamliners first introduced

1954

Railroads begin to offer piggyback service for freight

1970

Amtrak is created by the United States government

2000

Amtrak begins its high-speed Acela Express service

Places to Visit

Below is a list of railroad museums that display vintage locomotives, cars, and other railroad equipment. The museums also feature photographs and films depicting railroading activities. Many offer rides on trains pulled by historic steam locomotives.

Alabama

Huntsville Depot Museum
320 Church Street
Huntsville, AL 35801
800-678-1819
www.alabamatravel.org/north/hdm.html

California

San Diego Railroad Museum
Campo Depot
31123-1/2 Highway 94
Campo, CA 91906
619-478-9937
www.sdrm.org

Colorado

Colorado Railroad Museum
17155 West 44th Avenue
Golden, CO 80402
800-365-6263
www.crrm.org

Illinois

Chicago Museum of Science and
Industry
57th Street and Lake Shore Drive
Chicago, IL 60637
800-468-6674
www.msichicago.org

Michigan

Henry Ford Museum & Greenfield
Village
20900 Oakwood Boulevard
Dearborn, MI 48124
313-982-6100
www.hfmgv.org

New York

Empire State Railway Museum
70 Lower High Street
Phoenicia, NY 12464
845-688-7501
www.esrm.com

North Carolina

The National Railroad Museum and
Hall of Fame
2 Main Street
Hamlet, NC 28345
www.micropublishing.com/railroad

Pennsylvania

Railroad Museum of Pennsylvania
State Route 741
Strasburg, PA 17579
717-687-8628
www.rrmuseumpa.org

Texas

Age of Steam Railroad Museum
1105 Washington Street
Dallas, TX 73515
214-428-0101
www.dallasrailwaymuseum.com

Utah

Utah State Railroad Museum
2501 Wall Avenue
Ogden, UT 84401
801-629-8446
www.theunionstation.org

Further Reading

Bourne, Russell. *Americans on the Move.* Golden, Colo.: Fulcrum, 1995

Combs, Barry. *Westward to Promontory: Building the Union Pacific Across the Plains and Mountains.* New York: Crown, 1986.

Cushing, Raymond and Jeffrey Moreau. *America's First Transcontinental Railway: A Pictorial History of the Pacific Railroad.* Pasadena, Calif.: Pentrex, 1994.

Daniels, Rudolph. *Trains Across the Continent.* Bloomington, Ind.: Indiana University Press, 2000.

Fitzsimmons, Bernard. *150 Years of North American Railroads.* Secaucus, N.J.: Chartwell, 1982.

Halberstadt, Hans. *Modern Diesel Locomotives.* Osceola, Wisc.: Motorbooks, 1996.

Herring, Peter. *Ultimate Train.* New York: Dorling Kindersley, 2000.

Holbrook, Stewart H. *The Story of American Railroads.* New York: American Legacy, 1981.

Husband, Joseph. *The Story of The Pullman Car.* Grand Rapids, Mich.: Black Letter, 1974.

Jensen, Oliver Ormerod. *The American Heritage History of Railroads in America.* New York: American Heritage, 1993.

Johnston, Carole. *Trains West.* Sioux City, Iowa: Quixote, 1997.

Johnson, Lynne and Michael O'Leary. *All Aboard!: Images from the Golden Age of Rail Travel.* San Francisco: Chronicle Books, 1999.

North, Paul. *American Steam Locomotives.* New York: Bookman, 1988.

Potter, Jane. *Great American Railroad Stations.* New York: Preservation Press, 1996.

Schafer, Mike and Joe Welsh. *Classic American Streamliners.* Osceola, Wisc.: Motorbooks, 1997.

Seaver, Dean. *The Golden Age of Steam.* New York: Smithmark, 1996.

Welsh, Joe. *The American Railroad.* Osceola, Wisc.: Motorbooks, 1999.

Wheeler, Keith. *Railroaders.* Alexandria, Va.: Time-Life Books, 1973.

Wilmer, Frank N. *The Amtrak Story.* Omaha, Nebr.: Simmons-Boardman, 1994.

Index

Page numbers in *italics* indicate illustrations.

Martin W. Sandler is the author of more than 40 books. His *Story of American Photography: An Illustrated History for Young People* received the Horn Book Award in 1984. Sandler's other books include *America, A Celebration!, Photography: An Illustrated History, The Vaqueros: The World's First Cowmen,* and the Library of Congress American history series for young adults. An accomplished television producer and writer as well, Sandler has received Emmy and Golden Cine awards for his television series and programs on history, photography, and American business. He has taught American studies to students in junior high and high school, as well as at the University of Massachusetts and Smith College. He lives in Cotuit, Massachusetts, with his wife, Carol.

Other titles in the Transportation in America series include:

Galloping across the USA: Horses in American Life

On the Waters of the USA: Ships and Boats in American Life

Straphanging in the USA: Trolleys and Subways in American Life

Driving around the USA: Automobiles in American Life

Flying over the USA: Airplanes in American Life